D1035427

*P O E T S   A N D
P R O P H E T S*

Early English Poets

POETS AND
PROPHETS

A selection of poems by

Early
English
Poets

CAEDMON TO
THOMAS MORE

CHOSEN AND
INTRODUCED BY

RUTH
ETCHELLS

A LION BOOK

Tring • Batavia • Sydney

Selection and introductory text copyright © 1988 Ruth Etchells

Published by
Lion Publishing plc
Icknield Way, Tring, Herts, England
ISBN 0 7459 1387 3
Lion Publishing Corporation
1705 Hubbard Avenue, Batavia, Illinois 60510, USA
ISBN 0 7459 1387 3
Albatross Books Pty Ltd
PO Box 320, Sutherland, NSW 2232, Australia
ISBN 0 86760 926 5

First edition 1988

British Library Cataloguing in Publication Data

Early English poets.—(Poets and prophets).
 1. Poetry in English, 1066-1400 –
Anthologies
 I. Etchells, Ruth   II. Series
821'.1'08

  ISBN 0-7459-1387-3

Printed in Italy

CONTENTS

INTRODUCTION

No series illustrating the pilgrimage of Christian faith made by some of our English poets could be complete without at least one volume which included selections from Early English poetry. Indeed, some of our richest and most lyrical Christian verse is to be found in Anglo-Saxon and Middle English writing. In making the selection which follows, I have taken material from the earliest Anglo-Saxon hymns and sagas (such as those by Caedmon and the unknown author of 'The Seafarer') right through to the beginning of the Tudor age. I have even cheated a bit by allowing Thomas More to slip in right at the last, as a sort of commentary.

This, then, is the evolutionary period of the English language — from the heavily accented rhythms of Anglo-Saxon, through the Anglo-Norman period and Chaucer's shaping of diverse materials into a recognizable 'English' synthesis, right on to the point where English is ready for its great flowering in the Elizabethan age. We are talking about a period of at least seven centuries: from the earliest Christian writing in England, through to a time just before the Tudor dissolution of the monasteries and the establishment by Henry VIII of the Church of England.

What unites this poetry as much as anything is that it is written during the period when all that the people of England knew was one Church — The Holy (Roman) Catholic Church — whose centre was Rome and whose theology and metaphors the English held in common with the whole of Western Europe. The selection spans the 'age of faith' as it was commonly known. Even as Sir Thomas More was writing his prayer poem, the spirit of questioning and agnosticism which came with the Renaissance was beginning to make itself felt.

So the poems I have chosen require an effort of imagination, and a sympathetic openness to their priorities. At the same time, there is much in them that is extraordinarily challenging to our contemporary spirituality. For one thing, these Christian poets spend far more time pondering, reflecting upon and wondering at the mystery of the incarnation, crucifixion and resurrection of Christ, and far less in expressing the griefs and frustrations of humankind, than is the case today. The Christian story has power for them. So they tell and retell various parts of it, expanding it with lively and sympathetic detail.

The theology behind this pondering and retelling of the Christian story is stronger, clearer, and much less dislocate than our own. Men and women are God's creatures, accountable to him, and receiving at his hands whatever destiny in this life seems good to God. This is not a matter of envy or complaint, but of acceptance. What matters is the response to our destiny, whether happy or tragic. What makes the accepting possible is the fact that the focus is not on this world, but on the *eternal* destiny of the individual soul. Living and dying are seen in the context of the judgement. The heavenly law court is very real in most of these poems: the awful justice of God has to be faced.

Hence the power of the crucifixion poetry. The figure of Christ is represented in various images of saving, defending, restoring — many, though not all of them, scriptural. Effective contemporary images are used: of the knight's battle with the dragons, of the 'Jousting of Jesus' on the cross, and of the 'harrowing of hell' — Christ's release of souls from the dungeons of hell. Christ is seen as the knight who in love has 'won the fight' to redeem mankind; or as the king who is rebuilding the wall-stones of Man's Castle of the Soul (a splendid adaptation of scriptural language).

At the same time as these great triumphant images ring through the poetry, however, there are other themes which touch us more familiarly. *Timor mortis conturbat me:* the terror of physical death does haunt some of the poetry, and the phrase has remained, haunting our literature ever since. The tensions between the certainties of the Christian faith and the anxieties and distresses of this life provide a moving undercurrent, particularly in the later verse. Again, however, instead of being located largely in the poet's own subjectivity, they are expressed through meditations on — for instance — figures in the Christ story: and in particular in the figure of Mary the mother of Jesus. I have therefore included two poems on Mary, out of the vast range available.

The earlier poems emphasize Christ's strength and endurance, and God's power, rather than the warmer qualities of love, gentleness and compassion. But by the fourteenth century the emphasis is shifting. (It had shifted culturally with the whole emphasis in the arts on 'courtly love', and the fresh perception of the Virgin Mary as *the* Virgin Queen of the heavenly court.) So I have included two poems on the theme of love written even *before* Thomas More's moving prayer, which so richly takes up this theme and dwells on it in relation to the gentle fatherly love of God.

The final brief section is headed 'In Praise of God'. But in truth most of the poems could have been included here. For what characterizes so much of this earlier poetry is the strong affirmation of God's goodness: even if, as in poems like 'Deor' and 'The Wanderer', the affirmation is a somewhat gloomy endurance of the astringent nature of God's goodness, rather than any vivid sense of joy!

I have begun this selection, however, with a poem which seems to me to express the modern mind and the modern dilemma, as well as that of its own period, in a quite extraordinary way, and which thus provides a bridge between our own age and these writers so far back in our own past. It is called 'Wit wonders'; and its simple message is that the Christian faith is so totally impossible for the rational mind to accept, that reason fails: it is God alone who can teach 'reason' 'the reason' for this faith. Man's 'wit' is shackled by mere 'reason', and sinks beneath the burden. 'Belief' and 'wonder', those two right responses of mankind to God, alone can help.

The attempt to make human wit, in terms of 'reason', the only arbiter, is with us still. These poems, therefore, may briefly recover for us another age's experience of that same 'belief' and 'wonder': and with them a sense of the powerful reality of Christ's intervention in human life.

PROLOGUE

WIT WONDERS

A God and yet a man,
A maid and yet a mother:
Wit wonders what wit can
Conceive this or the other.

A God and can he die?
A dead man, can he live?
What wit can well reply?
What reason reason give?

God, Truth itself, doth teach it.
Man's wit sinks too far under
By reason's power to reach it:
Believe and leave to wonder.

Anonymous, from the British Museum Harley Manuscript.

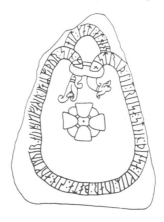

THE COMING OF CHRIST

nativity, crucifixion, resurrection, judgement

The Christian church's year begins with advent, in which Christians prepare themselves for the coming of Christ: both the 'coming' of his nativity, and that final coming of the last day, the terrible day, the day of judgement. As the Christian story begins, therefore, the themes of God's judgement and God's salvation are woven together.

ADVENT

I saw him with flesh all be-spread: He came from East.
I saw him with blood all be-shed: He came from West.
I saw that many he with him brought: He came from
    South.
I saw that the world of him ne rought: He came from
    North.

'I come from the wedlock as a sweet spouse that have my
    wife with me y-nome.
I come from fight as a stalwart knight that my foe have
    overcome.
I come from the cheaping as a rich chapman that
    mankind have y-bought.
I come from an uncouth land as a silly pilgrim that far
    have y-sought.'

From an anonymous manuscript in Merton College, about 1350.

Notes: be-spread: his body all spread out. *be-shed:* drenched. *rought of:* cared for. *have y-nome:* have taken. *cheaping:* market. *chapman:* merchant. *uncouth:* unknown. *silly:* innocent. *far . . . :* have travelled far.

You govern the locks, You open life,
O Lord and Ruler, righteous King.
Unless man's work is well done, You deny
him the paths of joy, the blessed journey.
Truly in our need we speak these words
and call upon Him who created man
that He should not consign to hell
those unhappy ones, we who sit in prison,
sorrowing. We yearn for the sun,
for the Lord of Life to show us light,
take our souls into His protection,
clothe our clouded minds in His glory;
we await the day when He will make us worthy
that He has admitted to His grace,
abject, cut off from our own country,
we who had to come to this narrow land.
Wherefore a man may say —
he who speaks the truth —
that, when it was lost, He delivered
the race of man. The maid He chose
for mother was still young, a virgin
without sin. The bride grew great with child
without once entering a man's embrace.
There has not been such merit in a woman
anywhere on earth, before or since;
it was a mystery, one of God's miracles.
All the gifts of the spirit grew on earth;
the Maker illumined many matters,
knowledge long since hidden under the soil;
the sayings of the prophets were realized
when the Ruler was born, He who fulfils
the cryptic words of those who, fittingly
and fervently, praise the name of the Creator.

From an adaptation of advent antiphons known as the 'Advent O's', about 820.

The notes of both suffering and joy which harmonize in the obedience of Mary are an inspiration for much Early English nativity poetry. Though the emphasis is on Mary's foreboding and heartache, yet she is also seen as the very Queen of Heaven through this same costly service.

NOW GOETH SUN UNDER WOOD

> Now goeth sun under wood —
> Me rueth, Mary, thy fairè rode.
> Now goeth sun under tree —
> Me rueth, Mary, thy son and thee.

Anonymous: from a Bodleian manuscript, 'Selden Supia', about 1275–1300.

Notes: Me rueth: I grieve for. *rode:* face.

I SING OF A MAIDEN

I sing of a maiden
    That is makèless:
King of all kingès
    To her son she ches.

He came all so stillè
    There his mother was,
As dew in Aprìllè
    That falleth on the grass.

He came all so stillè
    To his mother's bower,
As dew in Aprìllè
    That falleth on the flower.

He came all so stillè
    There his mother lay,
As dew in Aprìllè
    That falleth on the spray.

Mother and maiden
    Was never none but she;
Well may such a lady
    Goddès mother be.

Anonymous: British Museum manuscript, about 1450.

Notes: makèless: matchless, without a mate. *ches:* chose. *All so stillè:* as
silently.

Jesu, sweetè sonè dear,
On poorful bed liest thou here,
    And that me grieveth sore;
For thy cradle is as a bere,
Ox and assè be thy fere:
    Weep I may therefore.

Jesu, sweetè, be not wroth,
Though I n'avè clout ne cloth
    Thee on for to fold,
Thee on to foldè ne to wrap,
For I n'avè clout ne lap;
But lay thou thy feet to my pap
    And wite thee from the cold.

Anonymous: British Museum Harley Manuscript, about 1375.

Notes: poorful: wretchedly poor. *bere:* byre. *fere:* companions. *lap:* fold of garment. *wite:* keep.

$\boxed{C}$ hrist's passion is the most powerful source of Christian poetic inspiration in this period, from 'The Dream of the Rood' onwards. Priority of place has been given here to William Langland's great fourteenth-century poem 'The Vision of Piers Plowman'. The selected lines below mark the climax of the central part of the poem — the trial and crucifixion of Jesus. The serene 'Et Incarnatus Est' with which these excerpts end, is Langland's beautiful exposition of the meaning of the incarnation and the crucifixion.

The poem 'Woefully arrayed' is probably of later date, written possibly, though not probably, by John Skelton, some time in the fifteenth century.

THE JOUSTING OF JESUS

The dreamer, Piers, is speaking:

'Who shall joust with Jesus?', quod I, 'Jews or scribes?'
'Nay', quod he, 'the foul fiend and Falsehood and Death.
Death saith he shall fordo and adown bring
All that liveth or looketh on land or in water.
Life saith that he lieth, and layeth his life to wed,
That for all that Death can do within three days
To walk and fetch from the fiend the fruit of Piers the
    Plowman,
And lay it where him liketh, and Lucifer bind,
And forbeat and adown bring bale and death forever:
    O mors, ero mors tua!'

Then came Pilate with much people *sedens pro tribulani*,
To see how doughtily Death should do, and deem of
    them both rightly.
The Jews and the Justices against Jesus they were,
And all their court on him cried '*Crucifige*' sharply.
Then put him forth a piller before Pilate, and said,
'This Jesus of our Jews' temple japed and despised,
To fordo it in one day, and in three days after
Edify it eft new (here he stands that said it),

And yet make it as much in all manner points
Both as long and as large by loft and by ground.'

'*Crucifige*', quod a catch-poll, 'I warrant him a witch!'
'*Tolle, tolle!*', quod another, and took of keen thorns,
And began of keen thorn a garland to make,
And set it sore on his head, and said in envy,
'*Ave Rabbi!*' quod that ribald and threw reeds at him,
Nailed him with three nails naked on the rood,
And poison on a pole they put up to his lips,
And bade him drink his death-evil; his days were done.
'And if that thou subtle be, help now thyself,
If thou be Christ, and king's son, come down from the
    rood;
Then shall we leve that Life thee loveth, and will not let
    thee die!'
'*Consummatum est*', quod Christ, and commenced for to
    swoon,
Piteously and pale as a prisoner that dieth;
The Lord of Life and of Light then laid his eyes together.
The day for dread withdrew, and dark became the sun,
The wall wagged and clove, and all the world quavered.
Dead men for that din came out of deep graves
And told why that tempest so long time dured.
'For a bitter battle', the dead body said;
'Life and Death in this darkness the one fordoeth the
    other;
Shall no wight weet witterly who shall have the mastery,
Ere Sunday about sun-rising' and sank with that to
    earth.
Some said that he was God's son that so fairly died,
      Vere filius Dei erat iste, etc.

*From William Langland, 'The Vision of Piers Plowman', about
1330–1400.*

Notes: *layeth his life to life to wed:* stakes his life as a pledge. *piller:*
pillager, robber. *by loft and by ground:* above and below. *catch-poll:*
sergeant. *witch:* sorcerer. *for a bitter battle:* because of a bitter battle.
witterly: truly.

ET INCARNATUS EST

Love is the plant of peace and most precious of virtues;
For heaven hold it ne might, so heavy it seemed,
Till it had on earth yoten himself.
Was never leaf upon linden lighter thereafter,
As when it had of the fold flesh and blood taken;
Then was it portative and piercing as the point of a
   needle.
May no armour it let, neither high walls.
For-thy is love leader of our Lord's folk of heaven.

From 'The Vision of Piers Plowman'.

Notes: Yoten: poured out. *Fold:* earth. *portative:* light to carry. *let:* hinder.

Woefully arrayed,
My blood, man,
For thee ran,
It may not be nayed:
My body blue and wan,
Woefully arrayed.

Behold me, I pray thee, with all thine whole reason,
And be not hard-hearted for this encheason,
That I for thy soul's sake was slain in good season,
Beguiled and betrayed by Judas' false treason,
Unkindly entreated,
With sharp cords sore fretted,
The Jewès me threated,
They mowèd, they spitted and despised me
Condemnèd to death, as thou maist see.

Thus naked am I nailèd, O man, for thy sake.
I love thee, then love me. Why sleepest thou? Awake!
Remember my tender heart-root for thee brake,
With painès my veinès constrainèd to crack.
Thus was I defacèd,
Thus was my flesh rasèd,
And I to death chasèd,
Like a lamb led unto sacrifice,
Slain I was in most cruel wise.

Of sharp thorn I have worn a crown on my head,
So rubbèd, so bobbèd, so rueful, so red;
Sore painèd, sore strainèd, and for thy love dead,
Unfeignèd, not deemèd, my blood for thee shed;
    My feet and hands sore
    With sturdy nails bore.
    What might I suffer more
  Than I have suffered, man, for thee.
  Come when thou wilt and welcome to me!

Dear brother, none other thing I desire
But give me thy heart free, to reward mine hire.
I am he that made the earth, water and fire.
Sathanas, that sloven, and right loathly sire,
    Him have I overcast
    In hell-prison bound fast,
    Where aye his woe shall last.
I have purveyèd a place full clear
For mankind, whom I have bought dear.

*Anonymous (possibly John Skelton): British Museum Hailey
Manuscript, about 1450?*

Notes: wan: discoloured. *encheason:* cause. *mowed:* grimaced. *raised:*
scratched. *bobbed:* beaten or insulted. *unfeigned, not deemed:* in reality
and not in mere dreaming. *Hire:* service done expecting payment.

he theme of Christ as champion, Christ as victor, is
the over-riding idea in much early Christian verse in
English. One of the earliest expressions of this is found
in Cynewulf's 'Christ', written probably about the
eighth century. A popular legend, the 'harrowing of
hell', enshrined the notion that Christ descended into
hell to free the souls imprisoned there by the devil. (The
source of the story, which figured in the various cycles of
medieval mystery plays, is the apocryphal Gospel of
Nicodemus. The word 'Harrow' in Middle English,
meant 'rob'.) Langland's use of this legend is one of the
liveliest passages of 'Piers Plowman'. To bring out its
popular idiomatic raciness I have used the modern and
very free translation by Ronald Tamplin of parts of
Langland's account.

CHRIST THE VICTOR

Lo, the holy Hero-warrior, King of glory,
He the Helm of Heaven, hath arrayed the war
Right against His ancient foes, with His only might . . .

Now will He seek the spirit's throne of grace,
He, the Saviour of souls, the proper bairn of God,
After His war-play! Forward now, ye comrades,
Frankly march along! Open, O ye gates!
He will into you. He, of all the wielder, —
He, the City's King — He, creation's Lord,
Now His folk will lead, reft from the devils,
To the joy of joys, by His own victory.
'Twixt God and man He places a ghostly pledge
Of love — life's solace and of all light joy.

*From Cynewulf, 'Christ' (the section on the Ascension), about
eighth century.*

Hold still
Truth said: I hear some spirit
Speaking to the guards of hell,
And see him too, telling them
Unbar the gates. 'Lift your heads
You gates'
And from the heart
Of light
A loud voice spoke.
Open
These gates, Lucifer,
Prince of this land: the King of glory,
A crown upon his head
Comes.
Satan groaned and said to his hell's angels,
'It's that sort of light sprung Lazarus.
Unstoppable. This'll be big, big
Trouble, I mean all sorts of bother
For the lot of us. If this bigshot
Gets in he'll fetch the lot out, take them
Wherever that Lazarus got to
And truss me up quick as you like. Those
Old Jesus freaks and the weathermen
Round here have been going on about
This for years. Move yourself, Greaser Boy,
Get all those crowbars your grand-dad used
To hit your mum with. I'll put a stop
To this one. I'll put his little light
Out. Before he blinds us with neon
Get all the gates closed. Get the locks on
Lads, stuff every chink in the house.
Don't let pieces of light in! Windows,
Fanlights, the lot. Moonshot, whip out, get
The boys together, Horse and his lot
And stash the loot. Any of them come
Near the walls, boiling brimstone, that's it!
Tip it on top of them, frizzle them

Up like chips. Get those three-speed crossbows
And Ye Olde Englishe Cannon and spray
It round a bit – blind his Mounted Foot
With tintacks. Put Muhammad on that
Crazy catapult, lobbing millstones.
We'll stab them with sickles, clobber them
With those spiky iron balls on string.'
'Don't panic,' said Lucifer, 'I know
This guy and his shining light. Way back
In my murky past. Can't kill him off.
Dirty tricks don't work. Just keeps coming.
Still he'd better watch out, so help me.'
                    Again
            The light said unlock:
                Said Lucifer, Who
                    Goes there?
A huge voice replied, the lord
Of power, of strength, that made
All things. Dukes of this dark place
Undo these gates so Christ come
In, the son of heaven's King.
With that word, hell split apart,
Burst its devil's bars; no man
Nor guard could stop the gates swing
Wide. The old religious men,
Prophets, people who had walked
In darkness, 'Behold the Lamb
Of God', with Saint John sang now.
But Lucifer could not look
At it, the light blinding him.
And along that light all those
Our Lord loved came streaming out.

From William Langland, 'The Vision of Piers Plowman', about
1330–1400, trans. Ronald Tamplin.

The Christian faith which told with such vigour the legend of Christ robbing hell of its victims when he might himself have seemed its victim, was rooted in a powerful sense of the reality of Christ's resurrection. So we conclude this section with two examples of the exultant verse which expressed this conviction. In William Dunbar's poem (probably late fifteenth century), Christ is the victorious knight who has defeated the dragon and rescued its victims.

This victory is the precursor of the final victory when Christ returns in power, and the last judgement takes place. One of the earliest English Christian poems, the ninth-century 'Dream of the Rood' ('rood' means 'cross') describes both these victories. The cross of Christ tells its own story.

THE LORD IS RISEN

Done is a battell on the dragon blak,
Our campioun Chryst confountet hes his force;
The yettis of hell ar brokin with a crak,
The signe triumphall rasit is of the croce,
The divillis trymillis with hiddous voce,
The saulis ar borrowit and to the blis can go,
Chryst with his blud our ransonis dois indoce:
Surrexit dominus de sepulchro.

Dungin is the deidly dragon Lucifer,
The crewall serpent with the mortall stang,
The auld kene tegir with his teith on char
Quhilk in a wait hes lyne for us so lang,
Thinking to grip us in his clowis strang:
The mercifull lord wald nocht that it wer so,
He maid him for to felye of that fang:
Surrexit dominus de sepulchro.

He for our saik that sufferit to be slane
And lyk a lamb in sacrifice wes dicht,
Is lyk a lyone rissin up agane,
And as a gyane raxit him on hicht:
Sprungin is Aurora radius and bricht,
On loft is gone the glorius Appollo,
The blisfull day depairtit fro the nycht:
Surrexit dominus de sepulchro.

The grit victour agane is rissin on hicht
That for our querrell to the deth wes woundit;
The sone that wox all paill now schynis bricht,
And, dirknes clerit, our fayth is now refoundit:
The knell of mercy fra the hevin is soundit,
The Cristin ar deliverit of thair wo,
The Jowis and thair errour ar confoundit:
Surrexit dominus de sepulchro.

The fo is chasit, the battell is done ceis,
The presone brokin, the jevellouris fleit and flemit,
The weir is gon, confermit is the peis,
The fetteris lowsit and the dungeoun temit,
The ransoun maid, the presoneris redemit,
The feild is win, ourcummin is the fo,
Dispulit of the tresur that he yemit:
Surrexit dominus de sepulchro.

From William Dunbar, 'The Lord is Risen', about 1460–1520.

Notes: yeths: gates. *borrowit:* ransomed. *indoce:* endorse. *Dungin:* strike
down. *on char:* ajar, open. *to felye of that fang:* fail of his booty. *dicht:*
made ready. *raxit him:* raised himself up.

The cross is speaking:

Listen! I will describe the best of dreams
which I dreamed in the middle of the night
when, far and wide, all men slept.
It seemed that I saw a wondrous tree
soaring into the air, surrounded by light,
the brightest of crosses; that emblem was entirely
cased in gold; beautiful jewels
were strewn around its foot, just as five
studded the cross-beam. All the angels of God,
fair creations, guarded it. That was no cross
of a criminal, but holy spirits and men on earth
watched over it there – the whole glorious universe . . .

Now I command you, my loved man,
to describe your vision to all men;
tell them with words this is the tree of glory
on which the Son of God suffered once
for the many sins committed by mankind,
and for Adam's wickedness long ago.
He sipped the drink of death. Yet the Lord rose
with His great strength to deliver man.
Then He ascended into heaven. The Lord Himself,
Almighty God, with His host of angels,
will come to the middle-world again
on Domesday to reckon with each man.
Then He who has the power of judgement
will judge each man just as he deserves
for the way in which he lived this fleeting life.
No-one then will be unafraid
as to what words the Lord will utter.

Before the assembly, He will ask where that man is
who, in God's name, would undergo the pangs of death,
just as He did formerly upon the cross.
Then men will be fearful and give
scant thought to what they say to Christ.
But no-one need be numbed by fear
who has carried the best of all signs in his breast;
each soul that has longings to live with the Lord
must search for a kingdom far beyond the frontiers of this
world.

Now I look day by day
for that time when the cross of the Lord,
which once I saw in a dream here on earth,
will fetch me away from this fleeting life
and lift me to the home of joy and happiness
where the people of God are seated at the feast
in eternal bliss, and set me down
where I may live in glory unending and share
the joy of the saints. May the Lord be a friend to me,
He who suffered once for the sins of men
here on earth on the gallows-tree.
He has redeemed us; He has given life to us,
and a home in heaven.

*From Anonymous, 'The Dream of the Rood' Vercelle manuscript,
translation as in Crossley-Holland.*

THE APPOINTED DESTINY

In Anglo-Saxon verse the notion of each individual's personal destiny is dominant. What matters is not his fortune — whether a man is defeated in war or a homeless wanderer — but how he endures his destiny. What matters too, in *Christian* Anglo-Saxon verse, is that he should go to his fate guarded by faith in the angels of God and safeguarded by God's providence from the attacks of evil.

The extracts which follow are from three of the earliest English poems expressing some of these convictions. They are not specifically Christian poems, indeed they speak much more characteristically out of the themes of their Germanic past; but the conversion of England has taken place and it affects the conclusions to which the poets come.

'Deor' is one of the earliest poems. The minstrel poet briefly recounts a series of misfortunes famous in Old German heroic tradition, and comforts himself that, as these horrors passed, so will this. But the penultimate stanza goes beyond resigned endurance and has a clear Christian tone.

'The Wanderer', slightly later, is a dramatic monologue in which the speaker has lost, through his chief's death, protection and security, and wanders looking for a haven, never finding it, and pondering on life's transience. Comfort will come through facing vicissitudes in the right spirit, growing and achieving wisdom through using his 'share of winters in the world'. This bleak resignation and endurance is set in the framework of a prologue and epilogue which speak of a profounder Christian hope. It is this blend of old Germanic pagan stoicism with Christian hope that makes both 'Deor' and 'The Wanderer' so powerful.

The third poem, 'Waldere', consists of fragments but is

remarkable for some splendid lines of defiance between combatants, in which the appeal to God's mercy sounds the dominant note.

DEOR

The 'scop' (minstrel poet) is speaking:

> If a man sits in despair, deprived of all pleasure
> his mind moves upon sorrow; it seems to him
> that there is no end to his share of hardship.
> Then he should remember that the wise Lord
> often moves about this middle-earth:
> to many a man he grants glory,
> certain fame, to others a sad lot.
> I will say this about myself,
> that once I was a scop of the Heodeningas,
> dear to my lord. Deor was my name.
> For many years I had a fine office
> and a loyal lord, until now Heorrenda,
> a man skilled in song, has received the land
> that the guardian of men first gave to me.
>   That passed away, this also may.

Anonymous, about AD 700.

The hero Waldere is speaking to his antagonist:

Fetch this grey corselet from me, if you dare,
Ælfhere's heirloom covers these shoulders.
Well-meshed and effective, enriched with gold —
it is glorious war-gear altogether suited
to a prince who must guard his lifehoard
against enemies. It will not play me false
although bare-faced men have betrayed me again,
welcomed me with blades, as you yourself have done.
Yet He who is always active and wise
in all men's affairs can grant victory.
A man who puts his trust in the holy one,
in God for support, will be sustained in need
if he has made of his own life a sacrifice.

Anonymous, about AD 750.

Often the wanderer pleads for pity
and mercy from the Lord; but for a long time,
sad in mind, he must dip his oars
into icy waters, the lanes of the sea;
he must follow the paths of exile: fate is inflexible . . .

. . . When sorrow and sleep together
hold the wretched wanderer in their grip,
it seems that he clasps and kisses
his lord, and lays hands and head
upon his lord's knee as he had sometimes done
when he enjoyed the gift-throne in earlier days.
Then the friendless man wakes again
and sees the dark waves surging around him,
the sea-birds bathing, spreading their feathers,
frost and snow falling mingled with hail . . .

A wise man must fathom how eerie it will be
when all the riches of the world stand waste,
as now in diverse places in this middle-earth
walls stand, tugged at by winds
and hung with hoar-frost, buildings in decay.
The wine-halls crumble, lords lie dead . . .
'Here possessions are fleeting, here friends
    are fleeting,
here man is fleeting, here kinsman is fleeting,
the whole world becomes a wilderness.'
So spoke the wise man in his heart as he sat apart
    in thought.
Brave is the man who holds to his beliefs;
    nor shall he ever
show the sorrow in his heart before he knows how he
can hope to heal it. It is best for a man to seek
mercy and comfort from the Father in heaven where
security stands for us all.

Anonymous, about AD 850.

$\boxed{C}$ harms and spells are part of the attraction of early English verse. Here are two of Christian intention. The first is part of a 'Journey Spell' invoking safety in travel. The second is a 'Riddle', the answer to which is 'The Chalice'.

A JOURNEY SPELL

I guard myself with this rod and give myself into God's
　　protection,
Against the painful stroke, against the grievous stroke,
Against the grim dread,
Against the great terror which is hateful to each,
And against all evil which may enter the land.
I chant a charm of victory, I bear a rod of victory,
Word-victory, work-victory. May they be of power for
　　me . . .
I pray now to the God of victory, to the mercy of God,
For a good journey, a mild and gentle
Wind from these shores. I have heard of winds
Which rouse whirling waters. Thus ever preserved
From all fiends may I meet friends,
So that I may dwell in the Almighty's protection,
Guarded from the enemy who seeks my life,
Set amid the glory of the angels,
And in the holy hand of the Mighty One of heaven,
Whilst I may live in this life. — Amen.

*From a selection of 'Charms' (anonymous) in the Exeter Book,
about 800.*

St Eligius, AD 588–659, said in a sermon: 'But whether you are setting
out on a journey, or beginning any other work, cross yourself in the
name of Christ, and say the Creed and the Lord's Prayer with faith
and devotion, and then the evil one can do you no harm.

THE CHALICE

I heard a radiant ring, with no tongue,
intercede for men, though it spoke
without argument or strident words.
The peaceful treasure pleaded for mankind:
'Heal me, save me, helper of souls.'
May men understand the mysterious saying
of the red gold and, as the ring said,
wisely entrust their salvation to God.

From the ninety-six 'Riddles' (anonymous), Exeter Book, about 800–1000.

The last journey is the most fearful one. The prayer below is from one of the greatest heroic poems, 'The Battle of Maldon', spoken by a wounded warrior as he faced the death stroke. The same intercession marks the closing lines quoted from 'The Seafarer'; and 600 years later Dunbar and Audley are pleading from the same urgent need for help on that dreadful way.

F·R·O·M
THE BATTLE OF MALDON

The wounded Earl faces his death:

He yielded to the ground the yellow-hilted sword,
strengthless to hold the hard blade longer up
or wield weapon. One word more,
the hoar-headed warrior, heartening his men:
he bade them go forward, the good companions.
Fast on his feet he might not further stand;
he looked to heaven . . .

'I give Thee thanks, Lord God of hosts,
for I have known in this world a wealth of gladness,
but now, mild Maker, I have most need
that Thou grant my ghost grace for this journey
so that my soul may unscathed cross
into Thy keeping, King of angels,
pass through in peace: my prayer is this,
that the hates of hell may not harm her.'

Then they hewed him down, the heathen churls,
and with him those warriors, Wulfmaer and Aelfnoth,
who had stood at his side: stretched on the field,
the two followers fellowed in death.

Anonymous; fought AD 937 somewhere in the north-west of England.

THE SEAFARER

On earth there is no man so self-assured,
so generous with his gifts or so bold in his youth,
so daring in his deeds or with such a gracious lord,
that he harbours no fears about his seafaring
as to what the Lord will ordain for him.

Wherefore my heart leaps within me,
my mind roams with the waves
over the whale's domain, it wanders far and wide
across the face of the earth, returns again to me
eager and unsatisfied; the solitary bird screams,
irresistible, urges the heart to the whale's way
over the stretch of the seas.
                              So it is that the joys
of the Lord inspire me more than this dead life,
ephemeral on earth. I have no faith
that the splendours of this earth will survive for ever.
Though a man may strew a grave with gold,
bury his brother amongst the dead
with the many treasures he wished to take with him,
the gold a man amasses while still alive
on earth is no use at all to his soul,
full of sins, in the face of God's wrath.

Great is the fear of God; through Him the world turns.
He established the mighty plains, the face
of the earth and the sky above. Foolish is he
who fears not his Lord: death catches him unprepared.
Blessed is the humble man: mercy comes to him from
      heaven.
God gave man a soul because he trusts in His Strength.

Anonymous, from The Exeter Book, about 850.

TIMOR MORTIS CONTURBAT ME

I that in heill wes and gladnes
Am trublit now with gret seiknes
And feblit with infirmite:
    Timor mortis conturbat me.

Our plesance here is all vane glory,
This fals warld is bot transitory,
The flesche is brukle, the Fend is sle:
    Timor mortis conturbat me . . .

That strang unmercifull tyrand
Takis, on the moderis breist sowkand,
The bab full of benignite:
    Timor mortis conturbat me.

He takis the campion in the stour,
The capitane closit in the tour,
The lady in bour full of bewte:
    Timor mortis conturbat me . . .

Sen he hes all my brether tane
He will nocht lat me lif alane;
On forse I man his nyxt prey be:
    Timor mortis conturbat me.

Sen for the deid remeid is none
Best is that we for deid dispone
Eftir our deid that live may we:
    Timor mortis conturbat me.

Poem by William Dunbar, about 1460–1520.

Notes: Timor mortis conturbat me: The fear of death troubles me (Office of the Dead). *brukle:* feeble. *sle:* cunning. *campion:* champion.

Lady, help! Jesu, mercy!
Timor mortis conturbat me.

Dread of death, sorrow of sin
    Troubles my heart full grievously;
My soul it noyeth with my lust then —
    Passio Christi conforta me.

For blindness is a heavy thing,
    And to be deaf therewith only,
To lose my light and my hearing —
    Passio Christi conforta me . . .

Thus God he gives and takes away,
    And, as he will, so mote it be.
His name be blest both night and day —
    Passio Christi conforta me . . .

Oft with this prayer I me blest:
    '*In manus tuas, Domine;*
Thou take my soul into thy rest —
    Passio Christi conforta me.

Mary, mother, merciful may,
    For the joys thou hadst, lady,
To thy Son for me thou pray —
    Passio Christi conforta me.'

Learn this lesson of blind Awdlay:
    When bale is highest, then bote may be.
If thou be noyèd night or day,
    Say '*Passio Christi conforta me.*'

Poem by John Audley, Bodleian Manuscript, about 1426.

Notes: My soul it noyeth with my lust then: my soul is distressed by my
sinful desires then. *only:* especially. *mote:* must. *May:* maiden. *When bale
is highest . . . :* when trouble is at its height, the remedy may come.
noyed: troubled.

In the later part of our period, the images of the Christ who saves us are expanded to picture not only the dour and enduring young hero warrior king, or the chivalrous knight, but the 'meek and mild' one, the baby, and above all the figure of love. We therefore close this section with three of these later poems on Christ's redeeming of humankind's fate. The first is a short extract from 'Love true and ever green', written in the conventions of early mediaeval 'love carols', with reference to the flowers and showers of the natural world: but human love is found inadequate, and it is divine love for which the poet pleads. The second, 'Lullay, lullay, little child', is unique among lullaby carols sung to the infant Christ in that it is sung not by Mary but by a sinful human being for whom the baby is to die. The third, from the same source as the lullaby, brings together the images of the warrior here and the gentle suffering figure of love.

LOVE TRUE AND EVER GREEN

All other love is like the moon
That waxeth or waneth as flower in plain,
As flower that blooms and fadeth soon,
As day that showereth and ends in rain.

All other love begins with bliss,
In weeping and woe makes its ending;
No love there is that's our whole bliss
But that which rests on heaven's king.

An anonymous poem from about 1350.

Lullay, lullay, little child,
Thou that were so stern and wild,
Now art becomen meek and mild,
　　To save that was forlore.

But for my sin I wot it is
That Goddès son suffered this;
Mercy, Lord! I have done miss,
　　I-wis I will no more.

Against my Father's will I ches
An apple with a rueful res;
Wherefore mine heritage I les,
　　And now thou weepest therefore.

An apple I took of a tree
God it had forbidden me:
Wherefore I should damnèd be,
　　If thy weeping ne wore.

Lullay for woe, thou little thing,
Thou little baron, thou little king;
Mankind is cause of thy mourning,
　　That thou hast lovèd so yore.

For man that thou hast ay loved so
Yet shalt thou suffer painès mo,
In head, in feet, in handès too,
　　And yet weepen well more.

That pain us make of sinnè free,
That pain us bring, Jesu, to thee,
That pain us help ay to flee,
　　The wicked fiendès lore. Amen.

*An anonymous poem from Commonplace Book of Friar John
Grimeston, copied 1372.*

Notes: I-wis: certainly. *ches:* chose. *res:* rashness. *les:* lost. *If thy weeping
ne more:* if it were not for thy weeping. *so yore:* so long.

Love me brought,
And love me wrought,
Man to be thy fere.
Love me fed,
And love me led
And love me lettet here.

Love me slow,
And love me drew,
And love me laid on bier.
Love is my peace;
For love I chese,
Man to buyen dear.

Ne dread thee nought,
I have thee sought,
Bothen day and night,
To haven thee
Well is me,
I have thee won in fight.

An anonymous poem from the Commonplace Book of Friar John Grimeston, copied 1372.

Notes: fere: mate. *letter:* allows. *chese:* chose.

IN PRAISE OF GOD

This selection could not be complete without some examples of the songs of praise to the Creator God who provides for humankind. Caedmon's hymn worships the God who creates structure and order. In 'Christ the Cornerstone', Cynewulf develops the image from the Epistle to the Hebrews of Christ as the cornerstone of the whole edifice of God's people — seen here as a great mead-hall. 'O felix culpa', a much later poem, rejoices in God's good ordering, even of human frailty. And finally there are a couple of stanzas from Chaucer on the 'Love Unfeigned' of God, by which all false human loves should be tested.

CAEDMON'S HYMN

Now we must praise the Guardian of Heaven,
the might of the Lord and His purpose of mind,
the work of the Glorious Father; for He,
God Eternal, established each wonder,
He, Holy Creator, first fashioned
heaven as a roof for the sons of men.
Then the Guardian of Mankind adorned
this middle-earth below, the world for men,
Everlasting Lord, Almighty King.

From Caedmon, described by Bede in 'History of the English Church and People'.

CHRIST THE CORNERSTONE

O King! Thou art the wall-stone,
which of old the workmen
from their work rejected!
Well it Thee beseemeth
that Thou hold the headship
of this Hall of glory,
and should'st join together
with a fastening firm
the broad-spaced walls
of the flint unbreakable
all fitly framed together;
that among earth's dwellers
all with sight of eyes
may for ever wonder.
O Prince of glory!
now through skill and wisdom
manifest Thy handiwork,
true-fast and firm-set
in sovran splendour.

From Cynewulf, based on Advent 'O's antiphon 'O Rex Gentium'
(Advent Lyric III), about 820.

Adam lay y-bounden
   Bounden in a bond;
Four thousand winter
   Thought he not too long:
And all was for an apple,
   An apple that he took,
As clerkès finden written
   In theirè book.
Ne had the apple taken been,
   The apple taken been,
Ne haddè never our Lady
   A been heaven's queen.
Blessed be the time
   That apple taken was!
Therefore we may singen
   '*Deo Gracias!*'

Anonymous, from British Museum manuscript, about 1450.

TROILUS AND CRESEYDE

O youngė freshė folkės, he or she,
In which that love upgroweth with your age,
Repaireth home from worldly vanity,
And of your heart upcasteth the visàge,
To thilkė God that after his imàge
You made, and thinketh all n'is but a fair
This world, and passeth soon as flowers fair.

And loveth him, the which that right for love
Upon a cross, our soulės for to buy,
First starf, and rose, and sit in heaven above;
For he n'ill falsen no wight, dare I say,
That will his heart all wholly on him lay.
And since he best to love is, and most meek,
What needeth feignėd lovės for to seek?

By Geoffrey Chaucer, about 1385, ed. F. N. Robinson.

Notes: starf: died. *set:* sets. *n'il:* ne will.

EPILOGUE

To close I have chosen two poems, from the beginning and the end of the period, which together sum up much of the hope in adversity, longing for God and thankfulness for the gift of Christ, which we have seen in earlier pages. Thomas More marks a very clear transition to the modern world, standing at the point of Reformation in England, while himself so much a part of earlier tradition. With his moving and lovely affirmation of a personal relationship with God his Father we end this selection of the Christian verse of an earlier England. Bede, in the one vernacular poem ascribed to him, puts the question asked by so much Anglo-Saxon verse: Thomas More answers it with certainty.

BEDE'S DEATH SONG

Before he leaves on his fated journey
No man will be so wise that he need not
Reflect while time still remains
Whether his soul will win delight
Or darkness after his death-day.

From Cuthbert's account of Bede's death, about 735.

Grant, I thee pray, such heat into mine heart
That to this love of thine may be equàl;
Grant me from Satan's service to astart,
With whom me rueth so long to have been thrall;
Grant me, good Lord and Creator of all,
The flame to quench of all sinful desire
And in thy love set all mine heart afire.

That when the journey of this deadly life
My silly ghost hath finishèd, and thence
Departen must without his fleshly wife,
Alone into his Lordès high presènce,
He may thee find, O well of indulgènce,
In thy lordship not as a lord, but rather
As a very tender, loving father.

*From Sir Thomas More, 'Prayer of Pico' in 'Life of Pico', publ.
1510, written about 1504–5.*

As far as possible I have used modernized texts for the poems quoted, as collected in the following books: Helen Gardner, *The Faber Book of Religious Verse*, Faber, 1972 (FBRV in references below); Helen Gardner, *The New Oxford Book of English Verse*, OUP 1972 (NOBEV in references below); Hugh Martin (ed), *A Treasury of Christian Verse*, SCM 1959 (TCV in references below). *The Earliest English Poems*, translated by Michael Alexander (Penguin Classics 1966, 1977), copyright © Michael Alexander 1966, 1977 (EEP in reference below); Kevin Crossley-Holland (ed), *The Anglo-Saxon World*, OUP, 1984 (ASW in references below; extracts copyright © Kevin Crossley-Holland); Charles Causley (ed), *The Sun Dancing*, Puffin 1982, 1984 (SD in reference below).

The original texts preserving the manuscript spelling can be found in G.L. Brook (ed), *The Harley Lyrics*, Manchester University Press, 1956; J. A. W. Bennett (ed), *Piers Plowman*, OUP 1972; A. M. Kinghorn (ed), *The Middle Scots Poets*, Arnold 1970; F. N. Robinson (ed), *The Complete Works of Geoffrey Chaucer*, OUP 1957; Carleton Brown (ed), *Religious Lyrics of the Thirteenth Century*, 1932; *Religious Lyrics of the Fourteenth Century*, 1924; *Religious Lyrics of the Fifteenth Century*, 1939; W. B. Sweet, *Anglo Saxon Readings* (revised edn. 1967); J. A. W. Bennett and G. V. Smithers, *Early Middle English Verse and Prose*, OUP 1974 (revised).

Page 10 'Wit wonders' (FBRV)

Page 11 'Advent' (FBRV)

Page 12 'Advent Lyric II' (ASW) product of early ninth-century Mercia

Page 13 'Now goeth sun under wood' (FBRV)

Page 14 'I sing of a maiden' (FBRV)

Page 15 'The Virgin's Song' (FBRV)

Page 16 'The Jousting of Jesus', from *The Vision of Piers Plowman* (Langland) (FBRV)

Page 18 'Et Incarnatus Est', from *The Vision of Piers Plowman* (Langland) (FBRV)

Page 19 'Woefully arrayed' (FBRV)

Page 21 'Christ the Victor' (TCV) taken from the modernized version in *The Christ of English Poetry*, C. W. Stubbs.

Page 22 'Christ Harrows Hell' (SD) This very lively and free version of Langland, copyright © Ronald Tamplin, is quoted by Charles Causley in his 1982 anthology of Christian verse, *The Sun Dancing*.

Page 24 'The Lord is Risen' (NOBEV)

Page 26 'The Dream of the Rood' (ASW), early ninth-century Mercia (the second phase of Old English Christian poetry)

Page 29 'Deor' (ASW), unique in being an heroic poem with a lyrical form.

Page 30 'Waldere' (ASW), part of a much longer poem telling the Germanic legend of Walther and Hildegund, in flight from Attila the Hun.

Page 31 'The Wanderer' (ASW)

Page 32 'A Journey Spell'

Page 33 'The Chalice' (ASW)

Page 34 'The Battle of Maldon' (EEP)

Page 35 'The Seafarer' (ASW): Crossley-Holland writes, 'Together with *Beowulf*, probably the best known of all Anglo-Saxon poems . . . much more obviously the work of a Christian . . .'

Page 36 'Timor Mortis Conturbat Me' (NOBEV)

Page 37 'Passion of Christ Strengthen Me (FBRV)

Page 38 'Love true and ever green' (TCV)

Page 39 'Lullay, lullay, little child' (FBRV)

Page 40 'Christ's Love Song to Man' (TCV and FBRV)

Page 41 'Caedmon's Hymn (ASW): Crossley-Holland writes of this, one of the earliest fragments of Old English poetry, 'No less than 17 copies of *Caedmon's Hymn* survive, a clear indication that this short poem was particularly esteemed by later generations of Anglo-Saxons.'

Page 42 'Christ the Cornerstone' (Advent Lyric III, TCV) (This is in the same sequence of Antiphons as Advent Lyric II, from ASW (see page 12 above) but I have used the alternative translation offered by Hugh Martin as being more dramatic and striking.)

Page 43 'O felix culpa' (FBRV)

Page 44 'O younge freshe folkes' (FBRV)

Page 45 'Bede's Death Song' (ASW)

Page 46 'A Prayer' (FBRV)